DR JEKYLL & MR HYDE

2 actor version

Burt Grinstead
&
Anna Stromberg

from
Strange Case of Dr Jekyll and Mr Hyde
by
Robert Louis Stevenson

BROADWAY PLAY PUBLISHING INC
New York
www.broadwayplaypublishing.com
info@broadwayplaypublishing.com

DR JEKYLL & MR HYDE
© Copyright 2019 Burt Grinstead & Anna Stromberg

All rights reserved. This work is fully protected under the copyright laws of the United States of America. No part of this publication may be photocopied, reproduced, stored in a retrieval system, or transmitted, in any form or by any means, electronic, mechanical, recording, or otherwise, without the prior permission of the publisher. Additional copies of this play are available from the publisher.

Written permission is required for live performance of any sort. This includes readings, cuttings, scenes, and excerpts. For amateur and stock performances, please contact Broadway Play Publishing Inc. For all other rights please contact the authors c/o B P P I.

First edition: November 2019
I S B N: 978-0-88145-854-1

Book design: Marie Donovan
Page make-up: Adobe InDesign
Typeface: Palatino

This play is dedicated to Judy B, who knew more than anyone the power of acceptance and forgiveness.

DR JEKYLL & MR HYDE had its World Premiere between 6 June–29 July 2018 at The Davidson/Valentini Theatre at the Los Angeles L G B T Center (Produced by Blanket Fort Entertainment and Jon Imparato / The Los Angeles L G B T Center). The cast and creative contributors were:

JEKYLL/HYDE.. Burt Grinstead
everyone else.. Anna Stromberg

Director... Anna Stromberg
Sound design.. Burt Grinstead
Set design... Burt Grinstead
Lighting design..................... Matt Richter & Adam Martin
Costume design... Anna Stromberg
Stage manager.. Adam Martin
Stagehands...................... Dennis Peraza & Margaret Marx
Publicist............................Ken Werther / Ken Werther P R

DR JEKYLL & MR HYDE had its Off-Broadway Premiere between 6–15 December 2018 and 17 April–26 May 2019 at SoHo Playhouse (Produced by Blanket Fort Entertainment, Darren Lee Cole / SoHo Playhouse). The cast and creative contributors were:

JEKYLL/HYDE	Burt Grinstead
everyone else	Anna Stromberg
Director	Anna Stromberg
Sound design	Burt Grinstead
Set design	Burt Grinstead
Lighting design	Carter Ford
Costume design	Anna Stromberg
Stage manager	Carter Ford
Set builder	Terry Collins
Publicity	David Gibbs / DARR Publicity & Joe Trentacosta / J T Public Relations

CHARACTERS & SETTING

Player 1:
JEKYLL
HYDE

Player 2:
POOLE
UTTERSON
LANYON
SARAH
EXCITED WOMAN
DR CAREW
MADAME CAREW
OFFICER
ENFIELD
MAID
LITTLE GIRL
WOMAN
MAN
OLD WOMAN

1860's London

AUTHORS' NOTE

The strength of this play lies in its pacing. Pauses should only be taken when there's an ellipses or a "beat", and these should be brief.

It can be cast in a multitude of ways, but the original production was performed as a two-person play by the writers. One actor played the eponymous roles and the other played everyone else.

Parentheses indicate the continuation of a sentence that has been cut off by the other character.

As needed, physical attributes may be amended to fit the casting. Likewise, gender pronouns may be altered for casting, as well as names. Richardine Enfield may be Richard as was the case in the novella.

Scene 1

(Player 1, as JEKYLL, *stands center.)*

(Player 2, as EXCITED WOMAN, *stops behind* JEKYLL *and looks at the proceedings. She snaps open a fan and fans herself throughout the scene.)*

EXCITED WOMAN: Ooo. I just love a good execution. Don't you?

JEKYLL: Uh— This is my first.

EXCITED WOMAN: Really? Well, you're in for a treat. They really want to kill this one. You can feel the excitement in the air.

JEKYLL: Yes…

EXCITED WOMAN: Ooo. Here we go.

(Sound of a priest reading the last rites in the distance.)

EXCITED WOMAN: Ooo. We got such good spots as well. You can see the veins in the executioner's arms. Must be quite a heavy axe. It's crowded today, isn't it? Lucky we got this view.

JEKYLL: Right.

EXCITED WOMAN: Here it goes! Ooo. I can feel the butterflies in my stomach, can't you?

JEKYLL: Yes.

EXCITED WOMAN: He's raising the axe. I love it when he stops at the top, it's like he's teasing us. And…

(Axe chop sound. Excited Woman and Jekyll react in unison.)

EXCITED WOMAN: Oh...goodness me. I've never seen anything like this before. That criminal must have quite a thick neck.

(Axe chop sound again. JEKYLL *and the* EXCITED WOMAN *react.)*

EXCITED WOMAN: No. That one didn't get through either. Maybe they didn't sharpen the blade? Ooo. Here we go again.

(Axe chop sound. JEKYLL *and the* EXCITED WOMAN *react.)*

EXCITED WOMAN: Well. This is exciting, isn't it? I think that man's still alive. Three whacks, and he's still kicking. Looks like the executioner's quite angry now. Ooo. Here it goes—

(Axe chop. JEKYLL *and the* EXCITED WOMAN *react.* JEKYLL *looks sick.)*

(Axe chop. Axe chop. Axe chop. JEKYLL *and the* EXCITED WOMAN *react to each chop. After the last, they wipe blood off of themselves.)*

EXCITED WOMAN: Ooo. Goodness me. That was marvelous, wasn't it? I've never seen anything like that. My word. So bloody. And this is your first execution. What a lucky duck you are. Doesn't get much better, I tell you. I come to quite a lot of these.

JEKYLL: Right.

EXCITED WOMAN: This one certainly deserved it though. Evil, he was. Pure evil... So what brings you here this afternoon? Did you know one of the victims?

JEKYLL: No.

EXCITED WOMAN: Oh, that's too bad. I always enjoy talking to someone with revenge in their bellies. Oh, but you didn't know the murderer, did you? I can't imagine how someone like you—

JEKYLL: Yes.

EXCITED WOMAN: *(Talking over his answer)* —would know the mur— What's that you say? You knew him? The serial killer? The London Brute? The English Demon? The Beast of Regent Street?

JEKYLL: Yes.

EXCITED WOMAN: Ooo. Goodness me. How'd you know him?

JEKYLL: He is… He was my brother.

(EXCITED WOMAN *gasps and turns out to the audience in shock.*)

(Black out)

Scene 2

(Player 1, as JEKYLL, *stands center.)*

JEKYLL: Two types of man, ladies and gentlemen. There is good. And there is evil. Blast… *(He fidgets with his ascot in a mirror as he speaks. He can't quite get it right.)* Two types of… Good and evil. Think of the madman- Egad! I think I'm going mad. *(He starts over with the ascot.)* Think of the madman. He's been deemed incurable by all natural standards. I propose that this declaration is simply untrue. I believe I can cure— Blast blast blast blast blast! *(He gives up with the ascot.)*

JEKYLL: *(Calling offstage)* Poole?

(Player 2, as POOLE, *comes rushing in.)*

POOLE: Yes, sir.

JEKYLL: *(Referring to his ascot)* Can you? I'm a bit nervous.

(POOLE *starts to tie* JEKYLL's *ascot for him.*)

POOLE: Why's that, sir?

JEKYLL: I don't know. I just…I've been thinking about my brother.

POOLE: I don't mean to be insensitive, sir, but they did execute him *(Straight out to audience with great emphasis)* TWO YEARS AGO.

JEKYLL: I know, I know it was two years ago. It's just… Well, I don't think they're going to go for it.

POOLE: Who? And go for what, sir?

JEKYLL: The board. I don't think they'll approve my research.

POOLE: Ah, I see. Why do you say that?

JEKYLL: Well, I can't quite solve how to phrase it.

POOLE: Give it a go then.

JEKYLL: My speech?

POOLE: Maybe you just need some ears. *(She finishes the ascot.)*

JEKYLL: Thank you, Poole. Alright. Uh…

(JEKYLL *motions for* POOLE *to sit. She does, considering it a great honor.*)

JEKYLL: There are two types of man, good and evil.

POOLE: What do you mean?

JEKYLL: Well, I was getting to it.

POOLE: Oh, of course, sir.

JEKYLL: That was just the opening line.

POOLE: I see. Go on then.

JEKYLL: You don't think it's good?

POOLE: Well, I'm not sure yet.

JEKYLL: Just judging from that though.

POOLE: I suppose it might be a bit vague or a bit on the nose. Can't tell yet.

JEKYLL: Alright. How about I start with— ...The mind is split in two.

POOLE: Whose mind?

JEKYLL: All minds.

POOLE: I see.

JEKYLL: Was that not clear?

POOLE: Not just then.

JEKYLL: Alright... All minds are split in two.

POOLE: That's better.

JEKYLL: Thanks.

POOLE: Good and evil?

JEKYLL: Good and evil. Yes, that's what's next.

POOLE: Got it.

JEKYLL: Let me try again.

POOLE: Please.

JEKYLL: All minds are split into two parts. Good and evil.

POOLE: I like that.

JEKYLL: What?

POOLE: Parts.

JEKYLL: Just parts of it? Which parts? There's not much to section off yet.

POOLE: No. The part about parts.

JEKYLL: Oh. You like that?

POOLE: Yes.

JEKYLL: I've lost myself.

POOLE: That's alright. You can start from the top.

JEKYLL: Ah, I don't think they're going to go for it, do you?

POOLE: I haven't heard the speech yet.

JEKYLL: Right, but…

POOLE: Well, I would, sir.

JEKYLL: You would?

POOLE: Sure.

JEKYLL: Good and evil isn't too heavy-handed? I could say mad and sane, maybe.

POOLE: Good and evil feels biblical.

JEKYLL: *(Excited)* That's what I was going for!

(Doorbell chime)

JEKYLL: That's probably Utterson. Tell him I'll be right out.

POOLE: Yes, sir.

(POOLE *exits.* JEKYLL *looks at himself in the mirror.)*

JEKYLL: You can do this, Jekyll. You're a man of power and grace. You have power and grace.

(POOLE *re-enters.* JEKYLL *doesn't notice and continues his speech.)*

JEKYLL: They'll like your research because it's good research. They'll like you, because, well, you're put together and smart, and…dandy. You're a dandy chap. That's what you—

(POOLE *coughs.)*

(Beat)

JEKYLL: Was that Utterson?

POOLE: Yes. He's waiting outside for you.

JEKYLL: Thank you, Poole.

(POOLE *exits.*)

(*Light change*)

Scene 3

(*Player 1, as* JEKYLL, *and Player 2, as* UTTERSON, *stroll casually down the street at night.*)

UTTERSON: Dr Carew and his wife will be there. I'm not sure why Lanyon puts up with him. He's a snub-nosed, as they say, twit, if you ask me, and she's worse.

JEKYLL: Ah, Utterson. Carew's not that bad, and I think his wife is rather…

UTTERSON: I'm not speaking ill, Jekyll. You misunderstand me. Of course, I don't mind them myself, but I've heard people say such things. Just repeating what I've heard. Although, last weekend they invited me along to see L'étoile. Hilarious stuff. One of the particularly humorous moments where Lazuli spits at Laoula, I start splitting, as they say, ribs, and Carew starts to snicker. However, as soon as he does, Madam Carew gives him the look, you know the look I'm talking about, and he seals his lips as if they'll never part again. And that was act one. The rest of the play neither of them made a peep. Afterward, all they could do was talk about how funny it was. "Well," I said, "if you thought it was so damn funny, why not laugh?"

JEKYLL: (*Laughing*) What did they say?

UTTERSON: Oh, I didn't say it out loud. Who do you think I am, Jekyll?

JEKYLL: Right. Well, the theatre is no place to be entertained, Utterson. You know that.

UTTERSON: (*Laughing*) I suppose you're right.

JEKYLL: I should cut the joke from my proposal.

UTTERSON: Oh right, you're presenting that tonight?

JEKYLL: Yes.

UTTERSON: What was the joke?

JEKYLL: It wasn't funny anyway.

UTTERSON: *(Prodding* JEKYLL *in the ribs)* Come on! Spill!

JEKYLL: Alright, fine. It was, what do you get when you mix theology with science?

UTTERSON: I'm not sure. What?

JEKYLL: Madness!

(Beat)

UTTERSON: Ah. Yes. I see… Perhaps you should leave it out. Are you planning on going to Lanyon's birthday next week? He's really goin' for it with this one, he is. I can't find myself a costume. Renaissance themed. Who does he think he is?

JEKYLL: Right.

UTTERSON: Oh, did you hear Lanyon's daughter is back in town? That Sarah. She's quite clever and very charming.

JEKYLL: Right.

UTTERSON: She's had an eye on you for a long time, you know.

JEKYLL: Right.

(UTTERSON, *noticing that* JEKYLL *is lost in thought:)*

UTTERSON: Jekyll, you're an ugly, as they say, turd.

JEKYLL: Right.

UTTERSON: I see.

(Beat)

JEKYLL: Did you say something?

UTTERSON: No.

JEKYLL: Oh.

(Beat)

(Light change)

Scene 4

(Player 1, as JEKYLL, *stands downstage facing out, delivering his speech to the dinner party guests.)*

JEKYLL: Th-th-The human mind is a most confusing tool. With all its functions, it's, well, it's nothing short of incomprehensible. Its complex design allows us to process information that we see, hear, touch…smell… taste.

(Player 2, as LANYON, *pops out.)*

LANYON: Get to it, my boy.

JEKYLL: Right. Apologies, Dr Lanyon. My point is that it's impossible to study its inner workings. If we crack a head open and peek inside, all we'll see is, well, pink tissue. Your brilliant experiments with dissection have proven as much, right Dr Carew?

(Player 2, as DR CAREW, *pops out.)*

DR CAREW: Pink tissue. That's right.

JEKYLL: However, I have a theory. An age-old theory that dates all the way back to the time man first tried to answer to the question, "why am I here?"

(Player 2, as LANYON, *pops out.)*

LANYON: *(Making a joke)* I was about to ask the same thing, then I remembered this is my house, my dinner party, and I invited you! Ha!

JEKYLL: I'm sorry for the prolonged introduction to my research, Dr Lanyon.

(Player 2, as SARAH, pops out. Romantic music plays.)

SARAH: Let him get to his point, father.

JEKYLL: Thank you, Sarah… It's only that it's difficult to explain— (such a complicated yet simple theory)

(Romantic music cuts out. Player 2, as LANYON, pops out.)

LANYON: Only poking fun, my boy.

JEKYLL: Right. Well, my theory is simply that there are two main tracks of the mind. Good. And evil.

(Player 2, as MADAME CAREW, pops out.)

MADAME CAREW: *(To DR CAREW)* Evil? I think he is talking about his brother.

JEKYLL: No, Madame Carew. My brother has nothing to do with this conversation.

(Player 2, as UTTERSON, pops out.)

UTTERSON: He doesn't? I thought he was the whole idea behind this proposal? Didn't you tell me that just the other day?

JEKYLL: No, Utterson. This theory comes from simply observing human kind. People do good. And people do evil. Isn't that right, Madame Carew?

(Player 2, as DR CAREW, pops out.)

DR CAREW: What're you saying, Jekyll? Are you calling my wife evil?

JEKYLL: No. I think your wife is quite lovely.

DR CAREW: Now you are flirting with her?

JEKYLL: Not at all. I was just trying to establish a— (connection between what I was saying and her observation)

(Player 2, as MADAME CAREW, pops out.)

MADAME CAREW: Don't talk about me as if I'm not in the room. I'm sitting right here.

JEKYLL: Apologies, Madame. I was just responding to— (your husband's inquiry about my comment)

(Player 2, as DR CAREW, *pops out.)*

DR CAREW: I was defending your honor, my love.

JEKYLL: I feel as though I may have— (instigated something between you two)

(Player 2, as MADAME CAREW, *pops out.)*

MADAME CAREW: As if I cannot defend myself! Jekyll is as harmless as a bug on a leaf.

JEKYLL: Well, I'm in the room as well.

(Player 2, as DR CAREW, *pops out.)*

DR CAREW: I'm your husband. I do my duty as a man.

JEKYLL: If we can get back to what I was— (saying. I have quite a bit to cover.)

(Player 2, as MADAME CAREW, *pops out.)*

MADAME CAREW: You haven't done your duty in quite some time!

JEKYLL: Good and evil, ladies and gentlemen! GOOD AND EVIL! I refer to Matthew 8:28. Jesus casts demons out of madmen. I propose that with the right combination of chemicals we can cast evil from madmen as well.

MADAME CAREW: See? He is talking about his brother.

JEKYLL: No. I'll admit, Utterson was right. My brother may have influenced my reason for this research but— (he really doesn't have anything to do with my theory)

(Player 2, as LANYON, *pops out.)*

LANYON: *(Pronounces "Jekyll" as "Jee-kuhl" throughout the play)* Wait a minute, Jekyll. You're saying that you're Jesus?

JEKYLL: No. I'm saying that by using science— (we can cure evil)

(Player 2, as DR CAREW, *pops out.)*

DR CAREW: *(Finishing his sentence)* —we can cast out demons. Sounds like he's calling himself Jesus.

JEKYLL: I believe that we can cure evil.

(Player 2, as LANYON, *pops out.)*

LANYON: Like Jesus!

JEKYLL: No! Alright. Let me try this from a different perspective. I've heard that certain tribes in the Americas have been known to ingest herbs that opened up their minds and allowed them to experience a different reality. To them it was truth.

(Player 2, as DR CAREW, *pops out.)*

DR CAREW: Now he is speaking of drug use?

JEKYLL: No. I'm talking about ingesting the right combination of chemicals that can isolate the two main channels of the mind. Good and evil. Like I was saying. We all experience temptations, don't we?

(Player 2, as LANYON, *pops out.)*

LANYON: I don't. I'm a devout man, Jekyll. I resent the implication.

JEKYLL: I wasn't implying that— (you're anything but devout)

(Player 2, as DR CAREW, *pops out.)*

DR CAREW: Neither do I. Good Christians we are. Never been tempted in my life.

JEKYLL: Right. I've been testing the use of varied substances and their effects on the brain. I believe that we can separate and essentially break ties with those temptations entirely. We can be pure.

(Player 2, as SARAH, *pops out. Romantic music picks up where it left off.)*

SARAH: What was the truth then? Of which those natives spoke.

JEKYLL: I...don't know. But, but wouldn't it be fascinating to find out? I'm only proposing that— (the university give me a slight monetary sum)

(Romantic music cuts out. Player 2, as LANYON, *pops out.)*

LANYON: You're asking me for the university's financial support so you can act as God? Only God has the power to purify us, Jekyll. Surely you must be aware of that.

JEKYLL: Yes, but— No. I mean, I'm aware of that— (but that's not what I'm asking for)

(Player 2, as MADAME CAREW, *pops out.)*

MADAME CAREW: If you ask me, this all has to do with his crazy brother.

JEKYLL: No, Madame Carew. It doesn't. My brother was a man of God until his mind turned.

MADAME CAREW: And he started killing people.

JEKYLL: Yes. He did. But what if there was a way to stop that from happening!?

MADAME CAREW: I told you it was all about his brother.

JEKYLL: I'm not here to talk about my— (brother. I'm here to ask the for the university's support)

(Player 2, as UTTERSON, *pops out.)*

UTTERSON: *(Attempting to rescue* JEKYLL*)* We should toast! To the...to the future of the university.

JEKYLL: But I wasn't— (finished with what I was saying.)

(Player 2, as LANYON, *pops out.)*

LANYON: *(Raising his glass)* Here, here.

JEKYLL: I've already started some tests with— (different chemicals, but I need more funding)

LANYON: Let's not talk business anymore, Jekyll. Sarah's going to play us a song. Aren't you, bunny boo?

JEKYLL: Sarah plays?

(Player 2, as SARAH, *pops out. Romantic music picks up where it left off.)*

SARAH: Yes. I just learned how to play Toccata and Fugue in D Minor.

JEKYLL: Wow. That sounds lovely, but…if I can— (just get back to what I was saying)

(Romantic music cuts out. Player 2, as LANYON, *pops out.)*

LANYON: That's your favorite isn't it, Jekyll?

JEKYLL: Well. Yes, but— (Dr Lanyon, I'd like to finish what I was saying)

LANYON: Go play, Sarah.

JEKYLL: But, Dr Lanyon, I'd like to finish my proposal. I don't believe I got my— (fair share)

LANYON: Let's talk later my boy. Everyone make your way to the sitting room for some brandy and cakes. You coming, Jekyll? She learned the song just for you after all.

(Player 2 exits.)

JEKYLL: Yes. I'll be right there. *(He stands alone for a beat.)*

(Light change)

Scene 5

(Player 1, as JEKYLL, *stands center reading a book. Music and laughter can be heard from another room.)*

(Player 2, as LANYON, *enters.)*

LANYON: There he is. Sarah's wondering where you ran off to.

JEKYLL: I'm sorry. I wandered into your library by accident and got distracted.

LANYON: Quite the collection, isn't it?

JEKYLL: Yes, it is.

LANYON: What's that you have there?

JEKYLL: The Behavioral Psychology of— (the Chimpanzee)

LANYON: *(Overlapping)* —Psychology of the Chimpanzee? Funny little beasts, aren't they?

JEKYLL: Yes. I find their social interactions to be very similar to humans. Like how they show their teeth as a sign of aggression.

LANYON: *(Smiling a toothy smile)* Surely, you're not saying we're similar to monkeys, Jekyll?

JEKYLL: Of course not.

LANYON: About your proposal…

JEKYLL: Yes?

LANYON: I think the university…will have to pass on funding such a project.

JEKYLL: But Dr Lanyon—

LANYON: No buts. Unless you're talking about that of the Baboon. My word. Cute little red butts. It's page forty-three of that book there. Oh, if you like dense books, I think you'll find this one particularly heavy.

(LANYON *points to a book.* JEKYLL *picks it up.*)

LANYON: Open it up.

(JEKYLL *opens it.*)

JEKYLL: What?

(JEKYLL *pulls a gun from the hollowed-out book. Dramatic music plays.*)

JEKYLL: You have a gun?

(LANYON *takes the gun.*)

LANYON: Yes, of course. Not just brains, you know. Power as well. Fire power that is. *(Laughs at his joke)*

JEKYLL: Right. Well, I think this research could save lives—

LANYON: *(Waving the gun around)* Oh, enough about that, my boy. Dr Carew and I discussed the matter thoroughly.

JEKYLL: When?

LANYON: Just now.

JEKYLL: I only left the room a few moments ago.

LANYON: It only took a few moments. We feel that you may be too personally connected to this particular research.

JEKYLL: I'm a scientist, Dr Lanyon. I won't allow my emotions to affect me.

LANYON: It's a fool's errand, my boy. Proverbs One—

JEKYLL: "The fear of the Lord is the beginning of wisdom"?

LANYON: Yes. Good boy. Wisdom comes from the fear of God, not attempting to play God. Good and evil? Who do you think you are, Jekyll?

JEKYLL: I knew I should've said mad and sane.

LANYON: It wouldn't have made a difference. Some things are just not meant to be tampered with.

JEKYLL: But Doctor—

LANYON: No, enough of that, my boy! I'm in charge around here, and I don't want you toying with blasphemy. *(Points the gun at JEKYLL)* If you do, I will kill your career.

(LANYON makes a "bang" sound with his mouth, startling JEKYLL.)

LANYON: *(Laughing)* Put that away.

(LANYON hands the gun to JEKYLL. JEKYLL puts the gun away.)

LANYON: Now, come join the party. My daughter is looking for a dance partner.

JEKYLL: I don't dance.

LANYON: Everybody dances, my boy. See? *(Dances to the distant music)* The music is the puppeteer, and you are the puppet. Let it guide you.

JEKYLL: I see.

LANYON: Cheer up, my boy.

JEKYLL: I'll be right out. I just want to finish reading this essay about how chimps use physical contact as a sign of dominance.

LANYON: *(Patting JEKYLL's shoulder, hard)* Of course. Take your time. You're a good man, Jekyll. I'm happy to call you a friend.

JEKYLL: Thank you.

(LANYON goes to exit, then turns back.)

LANYON: By the way, my daughter is looking to be courted.

JEKYLL: Oh?

LANYON: So, do something about it, my boy. Quit monkeying around. *(Goes to exit again, then turns back)* Ha. Monkeying. Ha.

(LANYON exits laughing. JEKYLL stands for a moment and attempts to dance for a few beats. He stops, disappointed with himself.)

(Player 2, as SARAH, enters. Romantic music plays.)

SARAH: Am I interrupting?

JEKYLL: Oh no, Sarah. I'm sorry. I was just coming out to join the party.

SARAH: Oh. My father said you were waiting for me in here.

JEKYLL: Ah. Unfortunately, no.

SARAH: I see… Did you like my playing?

JEKYLL: Of course. It was…very pleasing to the ears.

SARAH: Thank you. I've been practicing all month.

JEKYLL: I do love that song.

SARAH: I know. I heard you say that at the last dinner my father hosted.

JEKYLL: Last month?

SARAH: Yes.

JEKYLL: I see.

(Beat)

SARAH: I liked what you said at dinner.

JEKYLL: You and no one else.

SARAH: They're just scared of you, Henry. It's alright if I call you Henry?

JEKYLL: It's fine.

SARAH: You're smarter than the lot of them combined.

JEKYLL: I don't know if that's true, but I appreciate the sentiment.

SARAH: I think so.

JEKYLL: Do you think I can cure evil?

SARAH: Of course.

JEKYLL: Really?

SARAH: Why not? It seems to me it could be like any other disease.

JEKYLL: Exactly. A plague, if you will. One that's made its way through us since the dawn of humanity.

(A romantic beat)

SARAH: What you said about temptations. Sometimes I have those. *(She edges closer to JEKYLL.)*

JEKYLL: We all do.

SARAH: You do as well?

JEKYLL: Of course. It's part of being human. The plague, so to speak.

SARAH: Do you think it'd hurt to indulge those temptations? *(She edges closer to JEKYLL.)*

JEKYLL: That's what I'm trying to cure. The overwhelming need to give in.

SARAH: What if— *(She edges closer still.)*

JEKYLL: Yes?

(JEKYLL turns and sees that SARAH is almost on top of him now.)

SARAH: What if I don't want to be cured?

JEKYLL: Ah, I see.

SARAH: Took you long enough.

JEKYLL: I appreciate your candor, Sarah, but I...can't. I have too much on my mind.

SARAH: I can help with that.

JEKYLL: Your father is my superior, and he's just in the other room.

SARAH: It's a library. You're supposed to be quiet in a library.

JEKYLL: I can't. It's not proper.

SARAH: No one will know.

JEKYLL: Yes, they will, and I'm an upstanding member of the faculty of the university. I'm a respectable man.

(Beat. This stings SARAH.*)*

SARAH: Are you saying I'm not respectable?

JEKYLL: No. Of course you are.

SARAH: Just because I want to become familiar with a man I'm attracted to doesn't mean I'm not respectable, Henry.

JEKYLL: That's not what I was saying. It's the circumstances that make it—

SARAH: Because I offered? It's not one I make lightly. I find you pleasing company, and I'd like to explore that further. Does that mean I'm no longer upstanding?

JEKYLL: *(Terrible joke)* Well. Technically, no. I assume we'd have been lying down.

SARAH: *(Sickened)* Ugh!

JEKYLL: Sorry. That was an awful joke.

SARAH: I thought you might be different.

JEKYLL: Different how?

SARAH: Not everything is good and evil, Henry. You're a slave to the rules set by people like my father. Like all of them out there. There's no truth in that.

JEKYLL: The truth is that we're slaves to base desires, like you just exhibited. I believe we can shake that!

SARAH: Why would you ever want that?

JEKYLL: Because… *(He holds up the book.)* We're not monkeys!

SARAH: No, we're not, but we're still animals, aren't we?

JEKYLL: We don't have to be!

SARAH: Yes, we do. It's what makes us human, and I happen to enjoy being human.

JEKYLL: You as well? I'm not trying to be God, Sarah.

SARAH: I should hope not! *(Beat)* I'm going to go get more wine. Would you like any or, should you be going?

JEKYLL: I…should be going. Tell your father thank you for having me.

SARAH: I will.

JEKYLL: I'm sorry.

SARAH: It's like you said, you've a lot on your mind.

JEKYLL: Yes… Perhaps?

SARAH: What's that?

JEKYLL: I've heard good things about L'étoile. Perhaps you could join me next weekend?

SARAH: Perhaps… Perhaps I'll have too much on my mind.

(SARAH *exits. Romantic music stops.*)

JEKYLL: *(To himself)* Perhaps.

(SARAH *re-enters. Romantic music plays again.*)

SARAH: I'll meet you at yours seven o'clock Saturday evening.

(SARAH *exits. Romantic music stops.*)

(JEKYLL *looks at the book he's still holding.*)

(Light change)

Scene 6

(Player 1, as JEKYLL, *sits alone in his house. He holds an empty glass.)*

(Player 2, as POOLE, *enters holding a package.)*

POOLE: Anything I can get you, sir?

JEKYLL: Do we have another bottle?

POOLE: Fortunately, that was the last one.

JEKYLL: I've only had a bit to drink, Poole. Don't be so judgmental.

POOLE: Right. I'm off to bed. *(Sets the package down.)* This arrived while you were out. It's from the Americas. Exotic looking thing.

JEKYLL: That'll be the herbs I requested. Bunch of money wasted. They threw out my proposal.

POOLE: I know. You told me when you came in.

JEKYLL: How could they do that? This research could change the world.

POOLE: Whose world, sir?

JEKYLL: Ah, I see what you're doing. It's not all about me, you know. My brother went mad. There's no changing that…but I can make sure it doesn't happen to anyone else.

POOLE: You could have, that is.

JEKYLL: Right. Before they threw out my proposal. Did I tell you they did that?

POOLE: You did, sir.

JEKYLL: Wait a hot minute. I don't need them! I have all the chemicals right here. I could—

POOLE: I'm not sure what you're thinking, Dr Jekyll, but I think it'd be best to think it over in the morning.

JEKYLL: Why's that?

POOLE: Where I'm from, nothing good ever comes from a decision made while stoned.

JEKYLL: Right. Well. Off I go to bed then.

POOLE: Goodnight then.

(POOLE *exits. Beat.* JEKYLL *grabs the package and takes it down into his laboratory.*)

(*Light change*)

Scene 7

(*Player 1, as* JEKYLL, *drunkenly mixes chemicals together. He holds the concoction to his lips.*)

(*He hesitates.*)

(*The following voices echo in his head.*)

LANYON: Only God has the power to purify us, Jekyll!

MADAME CAREW: If you ask me, this all has to do with his crazy brother.

LANYON: It's a fool's errand, my boy.

SARAH: Not everything is good and evil, Henry.

DR CAREW: Sounds like he's calling himself Jesus.

LANYON: Some things are just not meant to be tampered with.

(JEKYLL *lowers the concoction.*)

SARAH: Do you think it'd hurt to indulge those temptations?

(*Beat*)

(*He makes the decision.*)

(He drinks the potion.)

(A moment passes. Nothing)

(Then... He twists! He screams! He hunches over in pain!)

(Light change)

(Player 1 rises as HYDE. *He wears a big top hat.)*

(He looks at his hands.)

(He smirks.)

(He grabs a cane and exits the laboratory.)

(Light change)

Scene 8

(Player 1, as HYDE, *wanders the London streets at night.)*

(He exits. The following interaction happens off-stage. Player 2 is the voice of the LITTLE GIRL *throughout the scene.)*

LITTLE GIRL: *(Off stage)* One! Two! Buckle your shoe!

(Sound of HYDE *trampling over her.)*

LITTLE GIRL: *(Off stage)* OW!

*(*HYDE *enters.)*

HYDE: Watch where you're going!

LITTLE GIRL: *(Off stage)* OWWWEEE! I think I broke something!

*(*HYDE *doesn't look back.)*

(Player 2, as ENFIELD, *enters and stands in front of him, blocking his exit.)*

ENFIELD: You just trod over that girl there.

HYDE: No, I didn't.

ENFIELD: I saw you.

HYDE: She fell.

ENFIELD: You just ran right over her. You alright back there?

LITTLE GIRL: *(Throwing voice to sound like she's off stage)* I don't think my leg's supposed to bend that way!

HYDE: Out of my way.

ENFIELD: You're just going to leave her there?

HYDE: She's not my problem.

LITTLE GIRL: *(Throwing voice)* The bone's poking out of my leg!

HYDE: Let me pass.

ENFIELD: I'm a prominent member of this community, you know.

HYDE: I suppose that's a threat?

ENFIELD: You can't just injure a little girl and walk away as if she doesn't exist.

HYDE: She's fine.

LITTLE GIRL: *(Throwing voice)* I'm going to try to stand up! *(Screams. Throwing voice)* I'm just going to sit here.

HYDE: See? She's alright. Look. I live right over there.

ENFIELD: What's your name?

(HYDE *pauses.*)

ENFIELD: What are you trying to—

HYDE: Hyde. H...Y-D-E.

(Dramatic music plays.)

ENFIELD: Richardine Enfield. Pleasure to meet you, Mr Hyde.

(HYDE *doesn't shake* ENFIELD's *outstretched hand.*)

HYDE: *(Scoffs)* Pleasure?

ENFIELD: I can make your name stink around town. Now, it seems to me this little girl deserves some retribution. A financial contribution might ease the tension.

HYDE: Fine. How much would you like? *(He takes out a cheque book.)*

ENFIELD: It's not for me. It's for the girl's family. Does your family live around here girl?

(Player 2, unable to cover their face to throw their voice, looks around uncomfortably.)

ENFIELD: She must have fainted.

(HYDE hands ENFIELD a cheque.)

HYDE: Here. That should be sufficient.

ENFIELD: Quite a sum.

HYDE: Now, if I may pass.

ENFIELD: *(Reading from the cheque)* Hold on. I know this name. This is Dr Henry Jekyll's cheque.

HYDE: The money's good don't worry. *(He enters the back door to the lab.)*

(Lights change)

Scene 9

(Player 1, as JEKYLL, lies face down on the floor.)

(Player 2, as POOLE, enters.)

POOLE: I took the liberty of making you some tea, sir.

(JEKYLL rolls over painfully, gripped in a terrible hangover.)

JEKYLL: You're a goddess, Poole.

POOLE: More than that I think.

JEKYLL: Oh no. What did I do?

POOLE: You just could have warned me we'd have a guest staying here. I'd have made up the spare room.

JEKYLL: What's that?

POOLE: Mr Edward Hyde. Doesn't matter I suppose. Insisted on sleeping in the laboratory. Strange one that Hyde.

JEKYLL: He's down there now?

POOLE: I wouldn't know. He came in the back entrance last night. Scared me half to death. I went down with a kitchen knife, sayin' prayers, ready to die a horrible death at the hands of a mad robber, when that friend of yours—

JEKYLL: Hyde.

POOLE: Certainly wasn't hiding, that's for sure. Was standin' stark naked in front of a mirror, just admirin' his own—

JEKYLL: *(To himself, thinking)* Hyde.

POOLE: Right. And when I made my presence known, he just turned, casual as can be like. Didn't bother covering himself up or nothing. There it was…exposed. All of him. Just hangin' there. Not even trying to—

JEKYLL: *(To himself, thinking)* Hyde.

POOLE: Exactly. Didn't know what to do. But he explained that you invited him to stay for a while. Is that right? I didn't believe him at first, but he made a convincing argument, knew a lot about you. Would you like me to fill up the tub, it looks like you could use a dip in the—

JEKYLL: Poole?

POOLE: Yes?

JEKYLL: What did he look like?

POOLE: Well, I can't say for sure. I mean I saw all of him, but for some reason, he doesn't seem familiar anymore. He did leave a sick feelin' in me stomach though.

JEKYLL: I see.

POOLE: Will he be staying long?

JEKYLL: No. *(He turns, surprising himself.)* Yes. *(He turns back.)* No. *(He turns back.)* Yes. *(He faces* POOLE, *unsure, now.)* Maybe. Either way, he's a friend. Treat him as such…when you see him. I've given him a key to the lab. He'll probably come in and out of the back door as he pleases.

POOLE: Yes, sir.

JEKYLL: And Poole? Fill up that tub, please. I feel as though I smell like—

POOLE: Wet animal, sir.

JEKYLL: Have you been thinking that the whole time?

POOLE: It's quite pungent, sir. *(Exits)*

*(*JEKYLL *stands alone.)*

(Light change)

Scene 10

(Player 1, as JEKYLL, *stands downstage center speaking to the audience as his class.)*

JEKYLL: Thank you for reading that excerpt from Lotze's *Streitschriften*, Albert. Now, if you will all close your books, I'd like to add a quick preface to tonight's reading before you all make your way to Dr Carew's lecture on the dissection of the male reproductive system. *(He points to an audience member.)* That's not funny, Douglas. I believe that Lotze and other modern philosophers only go so far explaining the human condition. Their analysis of our mental capacity is truly magnificent, but what of emotions: happiness, sadness, anger, guilt, or love. I have a theory that compliments their ideas quite nicely. *(He stares at that same audience member.)* Douglas, no. It's not time to go yet. The greatest war that man ever experiences, is within his own mind. The battle between good and evil. I spent a number of years studying a boy with a head injury, little Georgie. Now, little Georgie had a large, very noticeable indent right here. *(He points to his forehead.)* Strangely similar to that of a soup bowl. Before this head injury, Georgie was quite a bothersome child. Trouble maker, if you will. Post trauma, however, little Georgie became quite agreeable. He wouldn't disobey. He wouldn't fight. He wouldn't cause any problems at all. I've studied many individuals with all types of head injuries, but none of them had similar results. A head injury here— *(He points to the back of his head.)* —and most become daft. Incapable of basic human functions. *(He glares at that same audience member.)* Douglas, eyes up here. Therefore, I theorize, as you all read in chapter four of my book, that the human personality, or the human soul, as it's been called, is located in the front portion of the brain. Now, in chapter five of my book, which I expect you all to read and annotate tonight, I retell the story of Adam and Eve from Genesis. When they took a bite of that fateful apple, as it says, they became aware of the knowledge of good and evil. Thus began the curse of man. Our twisted soul wrenched with two opposing forces. But, little Georgie was once thought to be the very definition of that latter force, evil, by all societal standards. And then, he fell out of a tree and was made good. Cured of the curse of man. Is it then possible that, with the right combination of chemicals, we can replicate Georgie's injury, without having a soup bowl indent right here? Is it possible for us to split the good side from the evil side? Maybe we can even destroy one of those sides altogether? I believe that it is within our grasp to create an antidote to that poisonous apple. To win the war that rages within our minds. *(He yells at that same audience member.)* Douglas! I only asked for a moment of your time. Am I not more interesting than whatever is written on that note you just passed to Albert? Don't answer that.

(Light change)

Scene 11

(Player 1, as JEKYLL, *is alone in his lab. He takes a deep breath, then lifts the serum to his lips.)*

JEKYLL: Let's see who you really are, Mr Hyde.

*(*JEKYLL *drinks it just as Player 2, as* POOLE, *knocks on the lab door.)*

JEKYLL: *(Choking on the serum)* Uh… Go away.

POOLE: Sorry to interrupt, sir, but Mr Utterson's here. *(Holds up a Renaissance costume)* I took the liberty of picking out some clothes for you to wear to Dr Lanyon's birthday party tonight. I have them here.

JEKYLL: *(To himself)* Eegad. That's tonight. *(To* POOLE*)* Uh… I don't think I can— *(He twists! He turns! He doubles over in pain! He screams!)*

POOLE: Everything alright down there?

(Player 1 rises as HYDE.*)*

HYDE: I'm fine.

POOLE: Sounds like you might be comin' down with a cold. Should I let Utterson know that you won't be able to make it to the Lanyon's tonight?

HYDE: No. I'll be right there. *(To himself)* Or rather, Hyde will be as Jekyll. *(He starts to laugh, maniacally.)*

POOLE: Sounds like a nasty cough you got. Are you sure you want to go?

HYDE: Yes, damn it! I mean— *(In a strained voice, trying to sound like* JEKYLL*)* Yes, Poole.

(HYDE *opens the door a crack and grabs the clothes from* POOLE.*)*

POOLE: Here you are, sir. I'll tell Mr Utterson you'll be right out.

HYDE: *(In the same strained voice)* Thank you, Poole. *(He closes the door and looks at the mask* POOLE *just handed him. He laughs maniacally again.)*

POOLE: Sounds quite bad, sir!

HYDE: Go away, Poole!

(Light change)

Scene 12

(Player 1, as JEKYLL, *wakes up in a hotel room wearing the Renaissance mask.)*

JEKYLL: What in the world… Where am I? *(He takes off the mask and looks around.)*

(Player 2, as the MAID, *knocks at the door.)*

JEKYLL: Who is it?

MAID: It's the hotel maid, sir. I'm supposed to clean your room now.

JEKYLL: Oh. Alright.

(The MAID *comes in.)*

JEKYLL: I was just leaving anyway.

MAID: Who're you?

JEKYLL: I'm... Why?

MAID: You're not the man what checked in.

JEKYLL: Who was it?

MAID: Ugly lookin' fella if you don't mind me sayin'. Went by the name of Hyde.

JEKYLL: I see.

MAID: Oh, by the by. The woman Hyde checked in with told me to tell him somethin'.

JEKYLL: What woman?

MAID: Don't know. Some woman.

JEKYLL: What was the message?

MAID: She said for Mr Hyde's ears only. *(She gestures for a tip.)*

JEKYLL: I can make sure he gets it.

(JEKYLL *pulls out some money. The* MAID *takes it, gleefully.*)

MAID: Alright. No harm done then, I s'pose. She said, she had quite a lovely time, and would like it to continue. She had to return home, but she'll meet that Hyde fella back here tonight.

JEKYLL: Oh no. Sarah.

MAID: No. I don't think it was no one named Sarah.

JEKYLL: Blonde?

(The MAID *nods.)*

JEKYLL: *(Gesturing with his hand)* About yea high?

(The MAID *nods.)*

JEKYLL: Warm eyes?

(The MAID *nods.)*

JEKYLL: Cute cheeks.

(The MAID *nods.)*

JEKYLL: Sarah.

MAID: No. That's not it.

JEKYLL: She looks a lot like you.

MAID: I suppose I could see that.

JEKYLL: Sarah.

MAID: She had a French accent if that helps.

JEKYLL: Madame Carew?

MAID: That's it. Carew.

JEKYLL: Blast! Sorry. Yes. It's seems that sometimes it's difficult to tell the difference between the two.

(Player 2 breaks character. She glares at Player 1.)

MAID: *(With the accent of the* MAID, *but the indignation of Player 2)* Really? I think the two seem quite distinct.

(Player 1 shrivels in discomfort. Player 2 continues as the MAID.*)*

MAID: Mind if I go 'bout my business now? Looks like that Hyde fella left me some nasty work.

JEKYLL: Please.

(The MAID *starts cleaning.)*

MAID: Can't even tell what fluid it is from these stains. How do you even get it on the walls, is my question? Look at that, it's on the ceiling as well. Oh, God! It's dripped on me. Oh God! Get it off! Get it off!

(Light change)

Scene 13

(Player 1, as JEKYLL, *sits alone in the living room.)*

(Player 2, as POOLE, *enters.)*

POOLE: Oh goodness me. You're home!

JEKYLL: Yes...?

POOLE: You've been gone for days, sir.

JEKYLL: I have? Yes. I have. I...went on a little trip.

POOLE: Does this have something to do with Hyde?

JEKYLL: *(Scared she knows)* What?

POOLE: Did that Hyde fella drag you along for some impromptu adventure?

JEKYLL: Oh. Yes. Yes, he did. Went to...the country.

POOLE: That why you smellin' somethin' fierce?

JEKYLL: Yes.

POOLE: I'll draw you a bath. Miss Sarah Lanyon will be arriving shortly.

JEKYLL: She will? For the opera. Of course.

POOLE: Are you alright, sir? You seem a bit nervous.

JEKYLL: *(Nervously)* I'm not nervous! You're nervous!

POOLE: Alright then. *(With a knowing smile)* Is it because of that Sarah? She's quite a catch, sir. I can see why you'd be a bit on edge.

JEKYLL: That's it. Yes.

POOLE: You'll be fine, sir. Just— *(Pats JEKYLL's shoulders.)* —be yourself.

JEKYLL: *(Weighing POOLE's words)* Right.

POOLE: Oh, Mr Utterson's here. He's come by every day talk to you about something or other. *(Exits)*

(Player 2, as UTTERSON, enters, still wearing part of POOLE's costume.)

UTTERSON: There you are, Jekyll. I've come by every day to talk to you about something or other.

(Player 1 breaks character and points to Player 2's costume. Player 2 looks down and removes the piece of the costume, embarrassed. They continue the scene.)

JEKYLL: I know. I just heard.

UTTERSON: First, you put on that bizarre show at the party. Then you disappear for days.

JEKYLL: I went on a little trip.

UTTERSON: Hyde?

JEKYLL: No, I'm not hiding anything. I really went on a trip.

UTTERSON: With Hyde? That's what I'm asking.

JEKYLL: Yes. With Hyde. Why?

UTTERSON: I've never met the man. Heard a lot about him, though. My cousin, Richardine Enfield, says he's quite the brute.

JEKYLL: Right.

UTTERSON: And yet, the two of you seem to be peas in the, as they say, pod.

JEKYLL: In a way.

UTTERSON: What has he got on you, man?

JEKYLL: What?

UTTERSON: Is it blackmail? Has he threatened you?

JEKYLL: What? No.

UTTERSON: Has he said he'd murder your friends? Am I in danger?

JEKYLL: Utterson, calm down. He's just an old friend. He's finally come out to visit, so to speak.

UTTERSON: Explain this, Jekyll. *(Holds up letter)*

JEKYLL: What's that?

UTTERSON: You don't know? The plot, as they say, thickens.

JEKYLL: *(Sneaking a peek at the letter)* It's a letter addressed from me to you.

UTTERSON: That's exactly what it is.

JEKYLL: And...?

UTTERSON: Did you write this letter, Jekyll?

JEKYLL: *(Unsure)* ...yes?

UTTERSON: Are you sure?

JEKYLL: *(Unsure)* ...yes?

UTTERSON: What's the first line say?

JEKYLL: ...Dear Utterson?

UTTERSON: Damn, you must have written it.

JEKYLL: May I see it?

(UTTERSON *hands* JEKYLL *the letter.*)

UTTERSON: I'm a respectable lawyer. I handled your mother's estate quite well if you ask me, but this? This, to me is an offense. You've promised this Hyde character everything. All of this.

JEKYLL: I see. *(Coming to a decision)* Yes. I did.

UTTERSON: Why?

JEKYLL: I don't have anyone else to give it to.

UTTERSON: You have your friends.

JEKYLL: Hyde is a friend. Closer to me than most, and if by some unnatural phenomenon I disappear, then Hyde should have control of all this. Now, I appreciate your concern, but if there's nothing else, I have get ready for my date.

UTTERSON: With Sarah? I'll get out of your, as they say, hair, but I would like to discuss this further.

JEKYLL: There's nothing more to discuss in this regard.

UTTERSON: I see. Tell Sarah I say, "Hello." She'll know what it means.

JEKYLL: I'm sure she will.

(UTTERSON *exits.*)

(JEKYLL *stands alone.*)

(*Light change*)

Scene 14

(*Player 1, as* JEKYLL, *and Player 2, as* SARAH, *sit next to each other in a box seat at the opera.*)

SARAH: I've heard wonderful things about this opera.

JEKYLL: (*Nodding*) Yes. Me too.

SARAH: The Carew's wouldn't stop raving about it.

JEKYLL: Right.

(*An awkward beat*)

SARAH: You're quite a dancer.

JEKYLL: I am?

SARAH: You were dancing up a storm at my father's birthday party.

JEKYLL: Yes, yes. It's practice. Years of practice.

SARAH: I didn't know you practiced dancing.

JEKYLL: It's a secret…that I just revealed to you. So, shhh, secrets.

SARAH: (*Giggling*) Shhh. Secrets.

JEKYLL: Yes.

(*Another awkward beat*)

SARAH: Something on your mind again?

JEKYLL: No. I mean, yes. I mean, it's nothing.

(Another beat)

SARAH: Why don't you ask me a question?

JEKYLL: About?

SARAH: Anything at all, start the conversation for once.

JEKYLL: Alright. Erm... What is your favorite activity for a lazy Sunday afternoon?

SARAH: *(Pleased)* That's a good one. I enjoy a good book, but more than that, I like to play music.

JEKYLL: You're very talented.

SARAH: Thank you.

JEKYLL: I could never play music. To me it seems so... tedious.

SARAH: *(Hurt, but she jabs back)* I suppose I feel the same way about playing with chemicals in a lab.

(JEKYLL *and* SARAH *share a smile.*)

SARAH: But, I don't know, there's something completely silent in music. I know that doesn't make much sense, but it gives me a sense of serenity, freedom. At the same time there's something quite loud about it. It can be chaotic, dangerous even. That Bach song you love.

JEKYLL: Toccata and Fugue.

SARAH: Yes. It's strong, powerful, angry, and at times overwhelming. Since you've introduced it to me, and my lazy Sunday afternoons, I haven't been able to stop playing it.

JEKYLL: You play it beautifully.

SARAH: Thank you.

JEKYLL: It takes a certain passion to hit the keys the way you do. Though, I believe, we all have it. That passion.

SARAH: You're saying I'm not special?

JEKYLL: No, no. You misunderstand—

SARAH: Relax, I'm joking. It's human to have passion, some of us just don't have the ability to focus it.

JEKYLL: Exactly.

(An awkward romantic beat)

SARAH: Alright. My turn to ask. What's your biggest fear?

(A beat)

JEKYLL: To be butchered alive by the executioner's axe.

(SARAH looks horrified.)

JEKYLL: Oh look. It's starting.

(Music plays.)

(JEKYLL sways happily to the music. SARAH sways as well, concerned.)

(Light change)

Scene 15

(Player 1, as JEKYLL, stands alone in his laboratory.)

(He's about to drink the serum again.)

(Player 2, as POOLE, knocks on the door to the lab.)

POOLE: Would you like some tea, sir?

JEKYLL: *(Startled and hiding the serum)* No, thank you, Poole.

POOLE: How was your night with Sarah Lanyon?

JEKYLL: Very nice, actually.

POOLE: Oh, you like her?

JEKYLL: I think so. Yes.

POOLE: That's wonderful, sir!

JEKYLL: Yes, it is.

POOLE: Needin' anything else tonight, Doctor?

JEKYLL: No. You can go to bed.

POOLE: Thank you, sir. *(Goes to exit)*

(JEKYLL *lifts the serum to his lips.*)

POOLE: Sir?

(JEKYLL *puts the serum down again.*)

JEKYLL: Yes?

POOLE: Will that Mr Hyde be coming back anytime soon?

JEKYLL: Yes. I believe he will. I'm growing quite fond of him.

POOLE: Oh, I see. Well, goodnight then. *(Goes to exit)*

(JEKYLL *drinks the serum.*)

(POOLE *turns around.*)

POOLE: Sir, I just wanted to say one more thing. You've been a wonderful employer, Dr Jekyll. I know you've been heartbroken about your brother these past few years, but you've still been very kind. You've been spending an awful lot of time in down there in your lab recently, and I'd, well, I'd hate to see you succumb to whatever it is you're going through. And I know this may be overstepping me bounds, but I think you need to get rid of that Mr Hyde.

(JEKYLL *twists!*)

POOLE: He's a bad egg that one.

(JEKYLL *turns!*)

POOLE: Worse even than your brother…

(JEKYLL *doubles over in pain.*)

POOLE: Don't mean no offense by that. I'll stop talking now. Goodnight, Doctor. *(Exits)*

(Player 1 rises as HYDE.*)*

HYDE: This is freedom, Jekyll. Freedom! *(He grabs his cane and exits.)*

(Light change)

Scene 16

(Player 1, as HYDE, *stands in the hotel room. Player 2, as the* MAID, *yells from off stage.)*

MAID: *(Off stage)* This is the room, sir.

(HYDE *hides. Player 2, as* DR CAREW, *comes careening on stage.)*

DR CAREW: Hyde! *(Pounds on the hotel room door hysterically)* You bastard! I'll kill you! *(Forces the door open looks around)* I know you were going to meet my wife here to- She told me everything! That's my wife, Hyde! You bastard! I'm here to kill you! You understand me! Where are you hiding, Hyde? *(Starts to cry.)* I'll kill you, Hyde. I'll kill you.

(HYDE *comes out of hiding.)*

HYDE: Hello, Dr Carew. Wasn't expecting to see you this evening.

(DR CAREW *goes to hit* HYDE. HYDE *dodges and grabs* DR CAREW.)

HYDE: No need for formalities, Doctor. Never any need for them if you ask me. If a man wants to eat, he should eat. If a man wants to drink, he should drink.

(HYDE *lets* DR CAREW *go.)*

HYDE: If a man wants to indulge in the pleasures of the flesh— *(He raises the cane in a phallic gesture.)*

DR CAREW: Now—

(HYDE *guides* DR CAREW *to his knees with the cane.*)

HYDE: —he should indulge. Formalities are only an illusion of respect, a waste of time, a gutless attempt at creating equality among the weak. The way you formally turned down my research proposal, for instance.

DR CAREW: But that was to...

HYDE: If a man wants to kill, he should kill, shouldn't he?

(DR CAREW *figures it out.*)

DR CAREW: Jekyll?

(HYDE *looks at* DR CAREW.)

HYDE: Oh no, we haven't been properly introduced. I suppose formalities are understandable behavior for that purpose. I'm Mr Edward Hyde. Pleased to meet you. That how it's done, right? What is it you say next? "The pleasure is all mine." Is that it? I'm speaking your language here, Carew. Then, I'd counter, wouldn't I? It's only polite to counter. "No," I'd say, "I assure you the pleasure is all mine!"

(HYDE *kills* DR CAREW *with his cane.*)

(*Light change*)

Scene 17

(*Player 1, as* HYDE, *walks casually down the street.*)

(*From off stage, Player 2, as the* MAID, *screams.*)

MAID: (*Off stage*) Oh my God! He's dead! He's dead!

(HYDE *starts to run. He runs faster and faster. He begins laughing maniacally.*)

(Light change)

Scene 18

(Player 1, as HYDE, *enters his lab through the backdoor. He drinks the serum.)*

(Player 1 rises as JEKYLL.*)*

(He walks up the stairs and exits his lab.)

(He walks over and opens a cabinet and pours himself a drink.)

(Player 2, as the OFFICER, *stands in his living room.)*

*(*JEKYLL *turns and screams at the* OFFICER, *startled by his presence. The* OFFICER *screams back.)*

JEKYLL: Detective! What are you doing here?

OFFICER: I'm sorry for the intrusion, Doctor. Your maid let me in.

JEKYLL: I didn't do anything.

OFFICER: Of course you didn't.

JEKYLL: What?

OFFICER: Is everything alright, Doctor?

JEKYLL: Fine.

OFFICER: Where did you just come from?

JEKYLL: Can I get you a drink?

OFFICER: Oh no, I'm quite alright. Still on the clock, you know.

JEKYLL: Right.

OFFICER: It's rather late, isn't it? What're you doing awake?

JEKYLL: *(Looks at his drink)* Research.

OFFICER: *(Referring to* JEKYLL's *drink)* Ah, I see. I've been known to do a bit of research myself from time to time. I'll put a stiff one inside me when I get home. Relax myself.

JEKYLL: Right.

OFFICER: Been a rough few days, but then I like it rough. It's the job I signed up for, catching bad men. Punishing them.

JEKYLL: I'm sorry. Why are you here?

OFFICER: There's a murderer on the loose. A man goes by the name of Edward Hyde. Looks a bit deformed, yet still quite handsome. Smells of wet animal, though. Very distinct. I've been after him for a few days now. Mr Hyde is quite the villain. Reminds me of your brother.

(JEKYLL, *conscious of his own stench, wanders to the other side of the room.*)

JEKYLL: You think he's like my brother?

OFFICER: Yes. Similar sense of madness. Just tonight, he killed a Dr Carew.

JEKYLL: Oh.

OFFICER: Did you know him?

JEKYLL: Yes. He was a…friend.

(*The* OFFICER *slowly makes his way to* JEKYLL *and puts his arm around him.*)

OFFICER: Hmm. I'm sorry for your loss. Well, don't be so hard on yourself, Doctor. As we used to say when I served in the military, "There's plenty out there that'll make it hard for you. No need to do it yourself."

JEKYLL: Right. Are you here tonight just to tell me about Dr Carew?

OFFICER: No, no, no. I'm here tonight because Mr Hyde was last seen around this neighborhood. We're warning all the residents. You've been a friend, Doctor. The Yard appreciates your assistance in the past, and we hate to ask it again, but if you have any information on this Hyde, or his whereabouts—

JEKYLL: I don't.

OFFICER: Of course. Either way, don't hesitate to be in touch. And, if you see my Hyde, I expect you to come, rather quickly.

JEKYLL: Yes. Of course.

OFFICER: I'll find him and bring him to justice if it's the last thing I do. He can be Mr Hyde, but I'll be Mr Seek. Oh, it's like the children's game. I love it when phrases have dual meanings. Goodnight, Doctor. *(Goes to exit. Sniffing)* Wait. What's that smell? Smell's like wet animal. *(He sniffs around, following the scent.)*

JEKYLL: *(Nervously)* I'm not sure...what that could be.

(The OFFICER *finally lands next to* JEKYLL.*)*

OFFICER: Oh, Doctor. That's really quite putrid!

(A beat)

JEKYLL: *(Fanning a fart)* I'm sorry. I thought you were leaving the room.

OFFICER: Oh, yes. Quite alright. Goodnight, Doctor. *(Exits)*

*(*JEKYLL *looks at himself in the mirror.)*

JEKYLL: What have you done now, Hyde?

(Player 2, as POOLE, *enters.)*

POOLE: Sir?

JEKYLL: Yes, Poole?

POOLE: I just want to let you know that I didn't tell them.

JEKYLL: Tell them what?

POOLE: That I heard someone come in the back door just before the coppers stopped by.

JEKYLL: What are you saying, Poole?

POOLE: I told you that Hyde was a rotten egg.

JEKYLL: That you did. Don't worry, I have a feeling he won't be coming 'round anymore.

POOLE: That's good, sir.

JEKYLL: In fact, can you take this? *(He pulls out a key from his pocket.)*

POOLE: *(Showing it to the audience, in an obvious manner)* The key to the back door, sir.

JEKYLL: Yes. We'll keep the back door locked from now on. Hyde won't be able to come in any longer.

POOLE: Goodnight, sir. *(Goes to exit but turns around)* Oh, and sir, I'll have you know that if I ever come across this Hyde fella again, I will immediately send for the police…or kill him meself if I have to.

JEKYLL: That's understandable, Poole.

POOLE: Goodnight, sir. *(Exits)*

(JEKYLL stands alone.)

(Light change)

Scene 19

(Player 2, as SARAH, and Player 1, as JEKYLL, are having a picnic in the park at dusk.)

SARAH: Terrible what happened to Dr Carew, isn't it?

JEKYLL: Right…I'm sorry. What was that, Sarah?

SARAH: Terrible what happened to Carew.

JEKYLL: Yes. It is.

(Beat)

SARAH: Something on that busy mind of yours, Henry?

JEKYLL: Yes.

SARAH: Would you like to talk about it?

JEKYLL: No.

SARAH: Oh… It's a beautiful sunset, isn't it?

(JEKYLL *doesn't respond.*)

SARAH: Why don't you ask me a question again? Start that conversation.

JEKYLL: Right. Alright. Why do you think you feel happy?

SARAH: In general?

JEKYLL: Yes. You seem like you enjoy life.

SARAH: What's not to enjoy?

JEKYLL: Well, everything I suppose.

SARAH: Hm. Well, the way I see it, there's two ways you can live life, Henry.

JEKYLL: Two?

SARAH: Happy or sad.

JEKYLL: That seems quite the simplification.

SARAH: It is, but no more than your good and evil.

JEKYLL: I suppose.

SARAH: It's quite easy to be sad. It comes naturally to us. And if you're looking for the world to be tragic, you needn't look far. It's quite a dark world.

JEKYLL: That it is.

SARAH: But if you focus on the darkness it will only grow and fester until it completely engulfs you.

JEKYLL: How can we avoid it then?

SARAH: Well, surely there are exceptions, but for me it starts by searching within myself. Finding my personal lens, let's say, through which I view the world.

JEKYLL: I'm not sure I understand.

SARAH: I'm saying you have to know who you are and be comfortable with that knowledge before you can look out.

JEKYLL: And you know who you are?

SARAH: Well, it's a daily search within, but I feel comfortable viewing the world through, well, me. And now, looking out, I don't see darkness anymore. I see flowers. I see sunshine. I see people smiling and singing. And when I don't see those things, I see rain, but I see it for the nourishment it brings the earth. I see dispirited faces as an opportunity to entertain with my music, or a chance to lift their frowns with some terrible jokes. I'm not saying you have to ignore the brokenness in the world to be happy, I'm saying you have to view it through a lens of…well, love.

JEKYLL: I see.

SARAH: Does that make any sense at all?

JEKYLL: Yes, unfortunately.

SARAH: Why unfortunately?

JEKYLL: I think we should stop seeing each other.

SARAH: What? Why?

JEKYLL: Because I have to accomplish that first step before I can enjoy this view, your company, or anything at all.

SARAH: What? I didn't mean to dissuade you from seeing me. Finding happiness is a much easier when two people are searching for it together.

JEKYLL: It's a little more complicated than that. Goodbye. *(He leaves.)*

(Light change)

Scene 20

(Player 1, as JEKYLL, *and Player 2, as* UTTERSON, *walk in the park.)*

UTTERSON: The town's a, as they say, buzz, Jekyll. It's been weeks, and no one seems to know where this Hyde character is.

JEKYLL: I know, Utterson, but I'll say it again. If I see him, I'll immediately send for the authorities. I can guarantee I won't see him, though.

UTTERSON: How can you be so sure?

JEKYLL: He left this note.

*(*JEKYLL *hands a note to* UTTERSON.*)*

JEKYLL: It says he's sorry for what he did, and that he left the country and is never coming back.

UTTERSON: I see. Looks similar to your handwriting, Jekyll.

JEKYLL: No, I'm a doctor. My handwriting is much sloppier.

UTTERSON: I suppose you're right. His picture's in all the papers anyway. He'd have a hell of a time showing his face around these, as they say, parts.

JEKYLL: Right.

UTTERSON: I threw out that other letter by the way.

JEKYLL: Right. Yes. Thank you. I'll stop by eventually and discuss who my real beneficiary will be.

UTTERSON: Absolutely. Take your time. You're young and healthy. I doubt anything'll happen anytime soon. *(A beat)* So, are you planning on seeing Sarah again?

JEKYLL: Well, I need to take time to myself right now. I need to get to know who I really am and what I really desire.

UTTERSON: You don't desire her?

JEKYLL: No, I do. I really do. She's wonderful. Perhaps too wonderful is all. I just—

UTTERSON: Is it a problem with your manhood?

JEKYLL: What?

UTTERSON: If you could develop a potion for that, it'd sell like, as they say, hotcakes.

JEKYLL: I don't need a potion for that.

UTTERSON: Right. Well, neither do I. I've just heard it's a problem. A very common problem. Among other men that is.

JEKYLL: Right.

UTTERSON: Oh, look over there. The theatre's playing something new. Perhaps we should stop by and collect the details.

JEKYLL: That's alright. I'm going to circle home if you don't mind.

UTTERSON: Oh, as they say, boo.

JEKYLL: 'Twas a lovely day for a walk, Utterson. I thank you for encouraging me to get out.

UTTERSON: A breath of fresh air can do a lot of good.

JEKYLL: Yes.

UTTERSON: Have a good day, Jekyll. *(Exits)*

(JEKYLL *sits on a park bench.*)

(*He spots a bird in a tree.*)

(*Player 2, as the* WOMAN, *enters and crosses in front of* JEKYLL.)

JEKYLL: Oh, look at you. You're quite a pretty little bird, aren't you?

WOMAN: Excuse me?

JEKYLL: Oh. No, there's a bird in the tree there—

WOMAN: Sure there is. (*She crosses off.*)

(JEKYLL *notices a cat in the tree.*)

(*Player 2, as the* MAN, *enters.*)

JEKYLL: Oh, no. Stay back you pussy.

MAN: Excuse me?

JEKYLL: No. There's a cat going after that bird in the tree there—

MAN: Sure there is. (*Walks off*)

JEKYLL: (*Watching the cat get closer to the bird*) Oh no! No!

(*Player 2, as the* OLD WOMAN, *enters and walks across the stage.*)

JEKYLL: Come to me. Here. You pretty, little thing! Come here.

(*The* OLD WOMAN's *ears perk up. She crosses to* JEKYLL.)

OLD WOMAN: (*Groping him*) I know my cue when I hear it. It's been a long time since a man's been so forward. Such a handsome one as well. Strong arms, look at that jaw—

JEKYLL: Madam! I'm sorry. There's just a bird in the tree there that—

(*The* OLD WOMAN *scoffs.*)

OLD WOMAN: Sure there is. *(She walks away. Mumbling angrily to herself)* Just trying to get a little something on the side. It never works out for me. *(She exits.)*

JEKYLL: The cat ate the bird. Blasted cat. *(He starts to shake.)* What's happening to me— *(He twists! He turns! He doubles over in pain.)*

(Player 1 rises as HYDE.*)*

HYDE: You can't Hyde me any longer, Jekyll!

(Player 2, as the OFFICER, *enters.)*

OFFICER: No, I will not, Madam!

*(*HYDE *covers his face and sits down, attempting to conceal himself from the* OFFICER.*)*

(The OFFICER *approaches* HYDE.*)*

OFFICER: Frisky old woman. I told her she was barking up the wrong tree. Hello, I'm Inspector Newcomen. I haven't seen you around these parts of the park before— Wait a minute, what's that smell?

*(*HYDE *stands up and turns around, facing the* OFFICER.*)*

HYDE: Hello, Inspector.

OFFICER: You're— I've got you now!

*(*HYDE *head-butts the* OFFICER.*)*

*(*HYDE *walks away, basking in his victory.)*

(The OFFICER *rises.)*

(They lock eyes. HYDE *runs!)*

(A chase ensues.)

*(*HYDE *pushes the* OFFICER *and exits.)*

OFFICER: *(To himself)* Come on, old chap. You can do this. You've spent your whole life training to be an officer of the law. You're stronger than he is! By Jove, you're going to catch that rat bastard if it's the last thing you do! *(Limps after* HYDE*)*

(Light change)

Scene 21

(Player 1, as HYDE, *roams through the London streets. He looks around, trying to keep his head down.)*

(Player 2, as the EXCITED WOMAN, *approaches.)*

EXCITED WOMAN: Oh, hello there. I heard there was a police chase happening over here. Quite exciting, isn't it? All these murders and now a police chase.

HYDE: Yes.

EXCITED WOMAN: I hope they catch him, so we can have another execution. Ooo, I'm giddy just thinking about it.

HYDE: *(To himself)* I have to become Jekyll. The chemicals in the lab! I don't have a key. Damn you, Jekyll. *(To* EXCITED WOMAN*)* Do you have a piece of paper, ma'am?

EXCITED WOMAN: Of course. Would you like one?

HYDE: Yes.

(The EXCITED WOMAN *opens her purse and searches for some paper.)*

EXCITED WOMAN: Wouldn't it be fun to meet the killer? Have a casual conversation with him about what have you, and never know that you were talking to the murderer? It'd be like meeting a celebrity, wouldn't it? Here you are, dearie.

HYDE: I suppose.

(The EXCITED WOMAN *hands* HYDE *a piece of paper. He pulls out a pen and starts drafting a letter.)*

EXCITED WOMAN: *(In a dreamlike reverie)* Ooo. Fantasy come true, that'd be. Then just when the two of you part ways, you realize that's the man they're looking for. Feels so dangerous just thinking about it.

(A police whistle sounds in the distance.)

EXCITED WOMAN: Ooo. Look at that. The police officers are coming this way.

(HYDE looks around concerned.)

EXCITED WOMAN: I wonder if the killer is around here somewhere. Ooo. Here they come.

(HYDE gets frantic. He looks at the EXCITED WOMAN.)

HYDE: Kiss me!

EXCITED WOMAN: What's that?

(HYDE dips the EXCITED WOMAN into a kiss. Amidst the kiss, Player 2 throws their voice as the OFFICER.)

OFFICER: *(Sounds as if it's off stage)* Oy! I'm going to get you, Hyde! If it's the last thing I do!

(HYDE brings the EXCITED WOMAN back up.)

EXCITED WOMAN: You smell delicious!

HYDE: Goodbye. *(He starts to run away.)*

EXCITED WOMAN: Wait a minute. Don't I deserve a name at least?

(HYDE stops, turns around, and bows.)

HYDE: I'm Edward. Edward Hyde. *(He exits.)*

EXCITED WOMAN: Hyde? The Hyde? The one they're looking— *(She can't cope with her excitement. She faints.)*

(Light change)

Scene 22

(Player 1, as HYDE, enters LANYON's courtyard and drops the letter he wrote in the previous scene. He hides.)

(Player 2, as LANYON, *enters, dancing to far off music.)*

LANYON: What's this? *(Bends down, awkwardly, and picks up a letter.)* "Dear Sarah. Please regard the following message with complete discretion. Do not let your father see this letter." Hmm. "And definitely do not read this out loud." Oh. *(Starts reading quietly.)* "A box that was delivered from the Americas..." "Mixed chemicals and herbs..." "a messenger..." "midnight." "In overwhelming gratitude, Dr Henry Jekyll." *(Looks around)* Jekyll? What is that boy up to? *(Exits)*

(HYDE *prowls through the audience.)*

(Light change)

Scene 23

(Player 2, as LANYON, *paces in his courtyard, clutching the package from* JEKYLL's *laboratory, filled with the chemicals from the Americas.)*

(Player 1, as HYDE, *enters.)*

HYDE: Dr Lanyon?

LANYON: Oh! You scared me. You must be the messenger. Jekyll's errand boy.

HYDE: Where's Sarah?

LANYON: She never got the letter.

HYDE: Damn it, Lanyon.

LANYON: I read it. Suspicious. I wanted to see what that Jekyll was up to myself. Very suspicious. *(Lifts up the package)* What is all of this?

HYDE: That's none of your concern.

LANYON: Wait a minute.

*(*LANYON *steps toward* HYDE. HYDE *steps back in response.)*

LANYON: I recognize you.

HYDE: The package.

LANYON: Your face.

(LANYON *steps toward* HYDE. HYDE *steps back in response.*)

LANYON: It looks so familiar.

(HYDE *turns away.*)

HYDE: Look, just give me the package. I'll bring it to Jekyll, and all this will be done with. I've nothing to hide.

(*Beat*)

LANYON: That's it! It's you, isn't it? Edward Hyde! (*Pulls a gun on* HYDE.)

HYDE: (*To himself*) Damn. Why'd I pick such an obvious name.

(HYDE *and* LANYON *standoff. They circle each other, pacing in unison.*)

LANYON: I knew I recognized your face. I've seen your sketch in all the papers. You're the man that killed Carew!

HYDE: No.

LANYON: Did you kill Jekyll as well?

HYDE: No! Give me the package, Lanyon!

LANYON: No!

HYDE: There are things happening here that you don't understand!

LANYON: Oh, shut up, you madman!

(HYDE *roars and lunges at* LANYON *grabbing the package.*)

LANYON: No! (*Beat*) Well, don't open it!

(HYDE *opens it.*)

LANYON: Don't take anything out of it!

(HYDE *takes out the chemicals.*)

LANYON: Don't mix them!

(HYDE *mixes them.*)

LANYON: Don't drink it!

(HYDE *drinks it.*)

LANYON: Blast.

HYDE: You've never been capable of understanding, you dimwitted, blustering, pathetic excuse for a doctor.

LANYON: Oh! You're just evil!

HYDE: *(Looking out at the audience)* Yes. Yes, I am. *(He twists! He turns! He grunts and doubles-over in pain.)*

(Player 1 rises as JEKYLL.)

(A beat)

LANYON: Jekyll?

JEKYLL: Hello, Doctor.

(LANYON *looks from* JEKYLL *to the package of chemicals, and back again. He clutches his heart.*)

(JEKYLL *holds* LANYON *as collapses to his death.*)

JEKYLL: Oh no! I'm sorry, Doctor Lanyon. I never meant for any of this to happen. *(He grabs his chemicals and runs away.)*

(LANYON *revives dramatically and writes on the back of the letter.*)

(A beat)

(He then rolls over and dies.)

(Light change)

Scene 24

(Thunder and lightning)

(Player 1, as JEKYLL, *stands in the rain. He knocks at* UTTERSON's *door. Player 2, as* UTTERSON, *enters in his pajamas.)*

UTTERSON: I'm coming, I'm coming. Hold your, as they say, horses. *(Opens the door)* Oh, hello Jekyll. It's quite late, isn't it?

JEKYLL: I know. I'm sorry to wake you.

UTTERSON: That's alright. How can I help you?

JEKYLL: Here.

(JEKYLL hands a collection of documents to UTTERSON.)

UTTERSON: What's all this?

JEKYLL: I set a new beneficiary for my estate.

UTTERSON: *(Joking)* Well, this is quite a suspicious time to be doing something like that. Are you planning on dying anytime soon? ...Jekyll?

JEKYLL: No. Of course not.

UTTERSON: Alright then. Respond a little quicker next time. Scared me half to, as they say, death.

JEKYLL: Go ahead and look it over. Sign at the bottom. It's you, and Poole. Split it up between the two of you.

UTTERSON: What's that?

JEKYLL: You're the only two friends that stayed with me through everything, and I expect you'll be the only two that remember me fondly.

UTTERSON: What's going on, Jekyll?

(JEKYLL starts to shake.)

JEKYLL: I...have to go.

UTTERSON: I don't like this.

(JEKYLL *grabs* UTTERSON's *hand.*)

JEKYLL: You don't have to, Utterson. It's out of your, as they say, hands. *(He leaves.)*

UTTERSON: But—

(Light change)

Scene 25

(Player 1, as JEKYLL, *paces around in his living room.)*

(Player 2, as SARAH, *enters. She watches him for a beat.)*

(JEKYLL *turns.*)

JEKYLL: Sarah? What are you doing here? Did Poole let you in?

(SARAH *holds* HYDE's *letter.*)

SARAH: What's this?

JEKYLL: I...don't know.

SARAH: I found it near my father's corpse. It seems to be a note from you to me, requesting to meet me at midnight with a box of chemicals.

JEKYLL: I—

SARAH: Even more suspicious, on the back of this note, my father seems to have scratched a collection of broken figures before he died.

JEKYLL: What?

SARAH: I believe it's meant to say, "Jekyll is Hyde." It's a strange case, isn't it? "Jekyll is Hyde." What do you suppose that means?

JEKYLL: I—

SARAH: No more secrets, Henry. No more lies.

(A beat)

JEKYLL: Remember my research proposal on good and evil? Well, I used myself as an experiment, and for the past month, I've lived two lives. Myself, that is, Dr Henry Jekyll and the other, a Mr Edward Hyde, a murderer, responsible for the death of Dr Carew, as well as your father's. I wanted to tell you, but I didn't know how, and now it's gone too far. I can't stop it. Hyde's inside me, begging to come out, and I want it. I want to be Hyde all the— You don't seem surprised.

SARAH: Listen to yourself. You want so badly for me to accept you, to sympathize with you. You've always been so wrapped up in being presentable by other people's standards, you've never been aware of what you were actually searching for... Once I interpreted my father's dying words, I sent for the police. I expect they'll be arriving shortly.

JEKYLL: No. *(He curls over in pain.)*

SARAH: You're evil, Henry. More evil than your brother, because you knew, didn't you? You ignited the fire, and you watched it burn. *(She pulls a gun and aims it at Jekyll.)*

JEKYLL: You don't understand! I can't hold him in any longer, and I'm out of the chemicals I need to control the transformations—

SARAH: And now you're too far gone to realize that Henry Jekyll is just as evil as Edward Hyde.

(JEKYLL *twists! He screams! Player 1 rises as* HYDE.)

(HYDE *knocks the gun out of* SARAH's *hand. It skids across the floor.)*

(HYDE *grabs her by the neck.)*

HYDE: You blithering whore! You've no idea what evil is!

(HYDE *chokes* SARAH. *He lifts her up in the air. She kicks in agony.*)

(*A beat*)

(*He twists!* SARAH *falls to the floor. He turns!* SARAH *rises. Player 1 rises as* JEKYLL, *but only for a moment. He twists again!*)

(*Player 1, now* HYDE *again, runs at* SARAH *and throws her to the ground.*)

(HYDE *looks at* SARAH. HYDE *goes after her. He twists! He falls back. Player 1 crawls on the ground as* JEKYLL.)

JEKYLL: Run! Go! NOW! I'm sorry!

(SARAH *runs.*)

JEKYLL: I'm sorry.

(*Light change*)

Scene 26

(*Player 1, as* JEKYLL, *paces his laboratory holding the gun.*)

(*Player 2, as* POOLE, *stands at the door to the lab.*)

POOLE: Sir? Everything alright down there?

JEKYLL: Did the package arrive from the Americas yet?

POOLE: No, sir.

JEKYLL: Then please keep the door locked.

POOLE: Is it alright if I come down, sir? Bring you some tea?

JEKYLL: No.

POOLE: Any food then?

JEKYLL: No, thank you.

POOLE: Is there anything I can do at all?

JEKYLL: You can stay away from me.

POOLE: I can't do that.

JEKYLL: Why not?

POOLE: Do I need a reason?

(A beat)

JEKYLL: Poole?

POOLE: Yes, sir?

JEKYLL: What does it mean to be good?

POOLE: That's a hard one to answer, sir. Depends on what you believe in. Though… Do you mind if I say something?

JEKYLL: Go ahead.

POOLE: Well, I don't think you should've been studyin' the brain.

JEKYLL: No?

POOLE: I think you should've been studyin' the heart.

JEKYLL: Why's that?

POOLE: I believe that's where it all matters. People can do good, and they can do terrible. But the important thing is…well, acceptance…and forgiveness.

(Sounds of police gathering outside.)

POOLE: The police are here, sir.

JEKYLL: Yes, I suppose they are.

POOLE: What would you like me to do?

JEKYLL: Keep the door locked.

POOLE: You should come out, sir.

JEKYLL: They'll kill me.

POOLE: You don't know that.

JEKYLL: They'll hack me up just like my brother.

(The police get louder outside.)

POOLE: There's a whole mess of them.

JEKYLL: I'm sure there is.

POOLE: Just come out, sir. It might not be as bad as you think.

(A beat)

JEKYLL: I turned him in. Did you know that?

POOLE: What's that?

JEKYLL: I told the police where he was.

POOLE: Your brother?

(A crash upstairs as the police force their way in.)

POOLE: You can still save yourself.

(JEKYLL convulses.)

JEKYLL: No! I can't. It's too strong. I can't—

(Sounds of the police get louder.)

POOLE: Yes, you can. Search your heart. Find the—

(Player 1 rises as HYDE.)

HYDE: I'll kill anyone that comes in here.

POOLE: No!

HYDE: Tell them!

POOLE: Come out or I'll come in, sir.

(Player 1 becomes JEKYLL.)

JEKYLL: Don't!

POOLE: I'm unlocking the door, sir.

(POOLE unlocks the door. Player 1 becomes HYDE.)

HYDE: Don't!

POOLE: I'm coming in!

(Player 1 becomes JEKYLL again.)

JEKYLL: Stop, Poole!

(POOLE *opens the door and descends the stairs.*)

(*Player 1, somewhere between* JEKYLL *and* HYDE, *stands for a moment, gun pointed at* POOLE.)

(*A long beat*)

POOLE: You've a good heart, Henry. Always have. Always will.

(*They look at one another.*)

(*A tense beat*)

(*He lowers the gun. He nods.*)

(POOLE *nods and slowly crosses to the stairs.*)

(JEKYLL *stands alone for a beat.*)

(*He turns the gun on himself.*)

(*Black out*)

(*BANG!*)

POOLE: NO!

END OF PLAY

www.ingramcontent.com/pod-product-compliance
Lightning Source LLC
Chambersburg PA
CBHW060216050426
42446CB00013B/3092